Gwen John Talking

– Stride –

Other books by the same author include:

POETRY:

Selected Poems 1951-1973 (Outposts Publications)
Browne Study (Lomond Press)
Dutch Comfort (Stride)
Jack o'Lent (Stride)
Leaving The Corner: Selected Poems 2: 1973-1985 (Stride)
Coeli et Terra (Cornerstone Press, USA)
Thames Listener: poems 1949-89 (University of Salzburg)

'City Whiskers' in *The Playing Of The Easter Music* (Stride)

Completing The Picture: exiles, outsiders and independents
[contributor] (Stride)
A Curious Architecture: a selection of contemporary prose poems
[contributor] (Stride)

FICTION:

Victoria Hammersmith (Stride)
London Clay (Stride)
The Bust Of Minerva (Oasis)
A Man In His Room (Stride)
The Servant Of His Country (Magwood)

PLAYS:

The Eagle And The Swan (Mitre Press)
Shrine Rites (Envoi Poets Publications)

EDITOR:

Palgrave: Selected Poems (Brentham Press)

CRITICISM:

The Fashioned Reed: the poets of Twickenham from 1500 (BOTLHS)

ABOUT THE AUTHOR:

Emotional Geology: the writings of Brian Louis Pearce
(A Stride Conversation Piece)

GWEN JOHN TALKING
Brian Louis Pearce

GWEN JOHN TALKING
Paperback (revised) edition 1996
© Brian Louis Pearce 1985, 1996
All rights reserved

ISBN 1 900152 09 6

Cover drawing © Ray Malone
Design by Joe Pieczenko

Acknowledgments
Acumen, New Poetry 9 (Arts Council),
100 Contemporary Christian Poets (Lion),
Coeli Et Terra (Cornerstone Press),
Completing The Picture (Stride),
Leaves For Palinurus (Downlander Publishing),
Leaving The Corner (Stride), *New Welsh Review*,
*Orbis, Ore, PEN Broadsheet, Pennine Platform,
Richmond Collage, Richmond Poets 1981,
Richmond Poets 1983, Stride,
Thames Listener* (University of Salzburg)
and *The Vigil*.

Gwen John Talking
was first published by Tallis Press in 1985.

*This new, revised edition
is published by*
Stride Publications
11 Sylvan Road, Exeter
Devon EX4 6EW

To Sir John Rothenstein
in appreciation of his *Modern English Painters*.

Contents

GWEN JOHN: SELF PORTRAIT

Peer at me,
probe me,
if you will.
Try me,
if you must.
I do not ask it
of you. I do not ask
you to come. I
do not ask
anything of you, or
of anyone, but
I await you,
hoping. Firmly
in command, yet
anxious, somewhat;
like an animal,
wary. Yet
strong, awfully
strong, at some moments,
surely.
Infirm, sometimes,
like the other women.
Some days the most blest,
at others the most un-
blessed of all women.
Why do I await you,
hope for you,
whoever you are?
Is it only
the visitation
of the one intense
and holy vision:
the coming of the one
supreme and over-
mastering idea
like the Annunciation
to Mary or the coming
to Abraham and Sarah
of the Strange One:

is it only for that
I wait here, half-
patiently, with only
the half of me here,
hour turning to day,
day drawing-out to year,
year becoming lifetime,
purifying myself?
Is it only for that
most holy First and Every-
Coming that I sit here,
alone in my bedroom, waiting?
Is it enough to wait here,
keeping faith with myself,
keeping my texture and
my surfaces clear:
lightening the brushstrokes;
intensifying, concentrating,
simplifying the vision, year
by year: looking
ever more understandingly,
yes, even like you, Rilke,
at the aura, the halo,
surrounding these things: yes,
these, the everyday things
that stand round me, peering
back at me, probing
hard at me, testing me
out, eyeing me, trying me
out thoroughly. Try me.
Yes, they are like prayers.
Let me name them over
as they watch with me, here:
jug, cup, table,
umbrella, shawl,
window, wickerwork chair,
simple bedstead, floor:
a few things but each
one my own, as I am.
I celebrate them, I
receive them with my fully

tiptoed, nude spirit, I
accept them, All-
in all, I
record them, as they are.
You, I declare to them.
These, I give to you,
these that I have lived for.
No. Not that dress,
not that brush, that book,
pencil, palette, easel,
but my own eyes, staring,
looking back, reflecting:
my own eyes, avoiding
cloth, table, window,
jug, cup, chair:
my own eyes, avoiding
anything but the self
behind them, needing to know
that self utterly, fully,
to see inside it and through it,
to probe it and to try it,
not one day, not
one hour, but for ever...
hammering... hammering... hammering...
on this frame of being
till I come to the open door.

A LADY READING

Standing, absorbed in her reading
the lady is busy translating
herself from an old Dutch painting.

Diminutive figure, enhancing
demurely the full skirt she's wearing,
keeping her eyes on her reading

she sees not the book but the meaning.
Her thoughts have flown out through the ceiling,
her soul has gone out through the door.

I think of her, still quietly standing
in the space made by her reading,
but my soul cannot find the same door.

SELF-AKIMBO

My arms akimbo, as I imagine Rimbaud,
unlike my elbow, my vision does not bend.
Poet, I leave you in limbo, beating your own *tombeau*.
I am my own hero, my all-sufficient end.
All my desires a *flambeau*, as I imagine Nero,
my furnace rages, and my fires extend.

A sense of braggadocio, panache,
otherwise foreign to me. Breast, hip, sheer
delight in sexuality, the lash
of this Welsh woman's presence thrust at you, voyeur,
or thrust at me, parched rider, ready to thrash
myself to frenzy and to taste my tear.

Almost, I'd come to inhabit the unreal
placebo-world you call the real; to inhabit
your thoughts instead of mine. I'm poised to steal
away, tell nothing, escape your trap, with the rabbit-
soul of me safe beneath my pose. I feel
it pulsate softly under this manly habit.

AUGUSTUS, IDA, THE SHADOW

Augustus, Ida, the Shadow,
and the beshawled infante:
it must be 1902.

I look like one of the hired
servants? You needn't tell me.
It's always the same. No one sees me,
there at the back, while my brother
is posturing about like the huntsman
sent to murder Snow White:
a taciturn outlaw, or sheriff
up against it, about to draw.
With that beard acting for him,
he could do anything, be
anything, brigand or prophet,
Brand or hired assassin,
a Montmartyred Bohemian,
anarchist, artist de luxe,
who cannot resist the enacting
of what is expected of him,
faithful in this, that he's wanting
his life to be one with his anecdotes.

Ida is holding the baby,
her meaning imaged in that.

Her sister-in-law, I am standing
(it was always the same) a little
behind them; a little, from where
I am standing, toward the left.
Did you know? Would you have guessed
that I was a painter, too?
Reticent, refusing apology,
I, too, have my stubborn streak.
I, too, have an untamed will.
Could you have guessed? Am I looking
like a lady in waiting
or a Princess Consort
dressed in clothes below stairs?

My life has been waiting and looking.
No one's eye is on me.
They are the actors: their's
is the stage, and the chief role.
The Shadow, I sidestep attention,
evading the cameraman's smile.
I'm nothing. But I turn back,
back to myself and my cats.
How can I keep up
with such a great black figure
sombrely standing there, brooding
in his black sombrero?
He overshadows everything
I am or try to do.
What is to be done
but hide and seek myself
in order to exist.

So that no one will see me
I stand up straight, to attention,
yet with such an intension
that sometime, somewhere, they will.
It is all necessary
so that I can achieve
my something, if only
I can be seen to exist.

This year, next year... always
round the corner: something
to be realised, somewhere;
not here, not yet, but still
as possible as ever:
this year, next year... this...

It is all necessary,
this seclusion, this posing,
so that I can exist.

MRS. ATKINSON

Oh, Mrs. Atkinson,
it's a long time to be
waiting someone, your son
come from the heavenly
mansions or the rent dun.

Ninety years in the parlour
dressed all in mourning, black
jacket, black hat, your pallor
seems like to see you crack
Boer War, Great War, in dolour.

Do you think of how show-
y you dressed to go out
walking with your best beau
once with pink scarf at throat,
before crinkles could show?

Your breakfasts are something
to be reckoned with. Egg,
bacon and toast, pot's sing
on the hob. Angels beg
your rooms in heaven, vying.

DORELIA IN A BLACK DRESS

brushing
past film-
y fern
in Avern-
us or
Kew

pushing
lost realm-
s of Eden
or Enitharmon
back into our
view

smiling
an apple
with branch
of olive
twined
serpently

beguiling
by ample
darkness, chance-
less below the grave-
cloths of the mind
folded patiently

but self-
con-
tained,
all com-
posure:
an

elf-
in one,
veined
handsome

by exposure
to man

the un-
yielded, myst-
erious musician
who never -- though bidden
often to embark —
got her viol wet

inviolate, un-
der the tongue, the chaste
but intense singer, fission
without fever, hidden
in March from Adam, dark-
er filmed than the violet

ETUDES

I
calm
am-
used
self
con-
tained
snoring
softly
waiting for
my
brother
to
finish
drawing

II
lamb
used
to the ram,
wilf-
ul and un-
explained,
looking
off, I see
pattern, floor.
Why
bother
to view
the fin of a fish
not worth the hooking?

III
come
tame
and abused

self
con-
strained
by a child's feeling
for the sisterly.
Hence for-
ward, I
am the brother
for who-
m I furnish
alms, healing.

IV

clothes
tight
buttoned
tickling
chin: hair down to
longish
nose:
broad
Ed-
wardian
hat
disguised with
feather
I chose

V

to prise a moth's
shut eye, opened
to the light
trickling
in like hoe-down to
melt the donnish
pose.
Bored
dead
the ward whose guardian-

's bat-
s with
leather-
y whiskers under his nose

VI

not of the Goths
but a quite
typically quiet-toned
Celt: liking
to grin while hairing into
it, that anguish
of a future none of us knows,
only to be clawed
back from the dead
by the God-warden
wat-
ching over our pith,
bringing it back from the nether
pitch where the quick-step slows.

VII

here I am
all aim-
ed, loosed,
up in my belf-
ry, bone-
d, brained,
clambering
aloft to the
trap-door
to try
to get to the other
side: to get through
before it vanish-
es, leaving me hammering

VIII

snow and sum-
mer time, I've mused
in this frame
of being, like a delph-
ic oracle, but un-
sustained
by any inspiring
tongue: cravenly
croft-bound, poor
in spirit, cry-
ing to smother
my fear of losing you,
this, and all the finish-
ed things, at my expiring

IX

home
Jame-
s, enthused
with yourself
and the one
true elite. Unrestrained,
the Huns are already roaming
the streets with their automata, deftly
bearing the four
figures of omen. I
sit on here, like a mother
where she last saw her child. Let the queue
move. I to the finish
sit still, intent on the one homing.

DEAR FIDDLER

Assurance is the theme
Gwen plays on, in the face
you select for us from
the ready-to-go-for-it, con-
fident, expectant rep-
ertoire you have prepared.
What executant aplomb
is putting those gloves on.

The scarf throws up its flame
on cheeks, lips, ears, a brown
study of background, jacket,
hat, gloves, hair. Breviary,
is it, tally or tale,
that book you have open
before you, though all set
to go out, as we see?

'I may never have any-
thing to express, except
this desire for a more
interior life', de-
clared your sister; yet she
stays on stage, as do you,
dear fiddler, whose encore
with the glove, jeu-d'esprit,

sees you adjusting your mood
so intently, in front
of us, Winifred, as though
existence' nub is today.
The score's before you. Prime
escort or ensemble offers
a part poised on a throw.
Go for it, Winifred; play.

CHLOE BOUGHTON-LEIGH

Can this person we see —
    hands loose, looking down — be
the real Chloe Boughton-Leigh?

Do the glum pose and cast feature
    mark the refuge of a resigned
spirit, a human creature

for whom experience
    has been drab-visaged, hence
the sad inelegance?

Is the face really Chloe's, so lit
    by the artist's own stoking and lined
by the matches our gaze strikes on it?

It is almost as if she were feeling
    her course to be fated, concealing
the rocks that the future's revealing.

Seen through the artist, she seems
    swamped by the waves, inclined
on her beam-ends, and best left to her dreams.

SELF-PORTRAIT NUDE, SKETCHING

All her subjects relate to herself. We see her
slender against the objects in a corner.
But it might be any object, any sitter.
It is always her we are shown, if we do not see her.

Every subject, an island in her ocean,
is subdued like clay, is given static motion
classical seeming, yet full of an emotion
proper to her, Romantic in self-devotion.

TO RODIN: THE WAVES

You know me by my silence

a silence and an absence

'the absence of all violence...'

How well do you know me?

Within me the violent waves
of emotion and agitation
surge to delivery, split
their sides with anguish, are flung
back but, slowly upheaving,
struggle to rise again, high
as on the Spring flood, and higher
until, at last, but how slowly,
they capsize and fall.

slowly, how slowly
         only
to emerge resurgent, early
rather than later; endlessly
ebbing and flowing, wearing
out the stones of my spirit:
busy about their rising
and my fall.
         Like first
love or an obsession,
continually they are
urging and concerning me
with their relentless surging
and their swell. Daemonic
for good or ill, these waves
that can inspire or destroy one,
curving with the fateful
attraction they hold for me, token
of my long-standing desire,
sudden, intense, passing,
returning or weary,

breaking me, splitting me, shaking me
to pieces upon them; rocking me
like flotsam from side to side:
knocking me against the breakwater,
tossing me up like seaweed
left to dry on the sand.
Angry, at times, yet a shadow
cast on a sea of shadows,
I am angry only inside.
You have seen nothing. You don't
know me. Yet, are you kind...
Ah, my friend, how fatherly
you are to me: how tenderly
you lay your chisel to me
disclosing the spirit folded
up in the stone of me, flawed
from my birth by my dullness.

I have but one choice. I must
choose that, despite these waves
that unsteady me still, that threaten
to engulf me... I,
who am all uncertainty, all
ungentleness, all impatience,
I must cling to my own image
whipped round in the whirlpool
of a lifetime's shadow and silence,
forced round by these waves.

Yet, it needs such patience.

Within me, I fell the waves
of my agitations, obsessions,
resume their remorseless and pauseless
probings deep down. From
the solitary unexplored depths of me,
rising through the immensity
of creation unseen and unknown,
I feel the shark's fin of my violence
cutting my surface, and swirling
darkly, out of control.

Do you not see it, there? Rising
half out of the water, then carelesssly
rolling lopsided below me,
it flops far beneath us again...

Whilst I work it is under...
it is just under control.

CREDO

I believe in the rushing wind, the tremendous driving force,
the sudden shaft, the sudden shifting of light, the interposition
of the Holy Spirit in these human affairs, the interpolation
of the tributaries, ponds and sources
                          the watery interfaces
water-sheds and water-forces
                    the sudden ripple of light
throwing diamonds across the water, turning
us to another quarter;
taking us round with the ebullient stream in another meander
into the presence of Godhead in these vessels of brittle clay:
the presence lighting these figures, otherwise fast disappearing
into a darkness deeper than any of their own making:
turning ahead of them, like the hidden water, and calling.

I believe in the wholly Other, the presence behind the mere clay of Creation:
the holy and solitary Father, who created us, by whom we are well met
in the terror and joy of this and every day,
in the middle of every instant
                    at the centre of every insight
at the first and last light of this and every I.

I believe in the grace which is daily searching and reaching us
which has to be felt to be seen, accepted to be believed,
and which, denied or acknowledged, has always inhabited us
from the first wrinkle across the ocean, as it ever shall be
in the day and the night-time, out beyond night, beyond day,
in the beginning, so, now, without end,
the sudden shaft, the ripple of light, like a person beside me,
nearer than hidden water
                turning to speak to me:
the sudden shift, the sound of the water
                turning

COMPOSITION

Choosing to go, needing to break away,
choosing not to choose between belief and art
but to oscillate between them;
breaking away, but only like a daughter
joyously to return, clapping my hands together,
cupping them with emotion,
holding my hands out for the wine, the bread.

You know my feeling, though deep, cannot be deeper
than anything you would know.
Why have I made you my master?
That feeling's at the front entrance; yet there's another,
round at the back-door, which persuades me I'm right
choosing to go, needing to break away.
Between the religion and the art, the balance

of fragile and precarious consciousness
that, weighed whilst weighing its own thought, is found
wanting and breaking down.
I reach up my hands to draw the pieces together.
Can I go on like this: breaking away
only to return; joyously
holding my hands out for the wine, the bread?

YOUNG WOMAN WITH BLACK CAT

Young woman
with black cat

black cat
with young woman

black cat
on lap

moves, is,
has weight

sniffs, settles,
listens, twitches

a whisker, pricks
an ear, blinks

its lids open, gleams
out in a green stream

hinting at summer in
the middle of shut-eye,

disposes felinity
comfortably, then

more comfortably
purrs like a low

undulation
of water growling

on stone, shifts,
licking its tail-fur

but, finally,
confident

the best position
for optimum comfort

is now known, sits
out the time there

with all its flopped weight
weighing the young human down

its presence substantial
unignorable: satisfied,

folds its claws, sighs
throbbingly, enters

a state almost
of grace, becomes

the silence, sits
unblinkingly still.

A NUDE GIRL

All that is human, racked and abortioning,
all that is maker, tightening, contortioning,
all that is Godly, redeeming, proportioning.

Maid of contrition, taut by immersion,
made of our flesh, the Divine in our version,
vestal like maker, your sex for conversion.

Distortion incarnate, mirroring man's mind,
negation of man-bearing motherly kind,
attenuation the maker has signed.

No word in the womb, no mothering meet,
no labour fulfilled; no 'It is complete';
no cry from the soul: *'Consummatem est'*, yet.

The womb-swelling word, from its first invention,
is dependent upon the Divine intervention,
but also, if fondly, on our tall intention.

First, if not last, it is these hips and haws
of yours that deny us, that still give us cause
to thrust and to question God's limits and yours.

Nude like your maker, stretched out by convention,
on the high wire without slackening of tension,
still Divine-bent, and still in contention,

with an ordeal to meet, an ideal to merit,
not yet intertwined with all you'd inherit.
An image for travailers. If it fits, wear it.

NUDE GIRL II

Like a pocket turned out, there, pathetically
offering what none has desired,

leaving still open a vacancy
for which not a body's enquired:

turned inside out, she is empty
like a room that was never required.

THE CONVALESCENT

That chair again, that table.
At least, they are something stable
in the amorphous flux, the watery world
of interflowing pigment, fluid ideas,
such as the artist has, and the convalescent,
when neither are at their most inspired or able.
The convalescent looks down. Her spirit seems curled
in on itself: accepting, acquiescent.
Where is the artist? Is it she who appears
in the sitter's face? Who is it has set the table?

She reads, but is reading nothing.
She looks, but is seeing nothing.
She wears the garment of simplicity
selected by an eye that sees itself
and everything it looks at as dependent
upon a single idea, one way of thinking.
An eye, a mind, locked in opacity,
turning aside, ungovernable, independent
of anything, it seems, except that self
which pictures, for a subject, its own looking.

If the sitter has life
it is alien. No if-
or-but of friendship or too sharply drawn
cup on the table is allowed intrusion
between the mind at the easel and its vision.
Which is more full of life, the cry and strife,
like tom-cats, of the town below, the horn
of taxi, van, the bellow or revision
of anarchical or republican confusion,
or one quiet spirit whetted like a knife?

STUDY OF A SEATED NUDE GIRL

As with De Chirico's mannikins, we are moved
by the juxtaposition of the bodily form
with the geometrical canvas's straight-edged norm:
the rectilinear figure that with the grooved
mathematical precision of a Mondrian wins
the attention of the intellect, though the features
are no more delineated than the creatures
of Dali or De Chirico's mannikins.

TO VÈRA OUMANÇOFF

To me, it is always the last day;
that's why I never look forward,
or see it all quite like the others:
that's why I'm different — I'm odd.

Immediate things, like these grasses,
the flowers in the wood, like these bluebells;
the cats that walk through my country,
like the orphans in church, neatly shod,

wearing black hats and white collars,
that I crouch drawing at Vespers:
these are my objects of worship,
the chattering small-talk of God.

GWEN JOHN TALKING

Sitting up here in this attic,
under the slope of the eaves...
sitting by the closed window,
I look – down and out – on the passers...
a cat on my lap, an old clock
ticking away on the dresser...
happier than any old widow
who has lost husband or senses.
This basket chair is my husband...
the cat on my lap is my child.
These brushes end my adventure
as they began it at Tenby.
The image we make is our spouse.

I set the cat on the lap
of a quite imaginary pal.
Tonks thought her drawing showed promise.
Wait there, while I wash out my palette.
Not the polished precision
that Ambrose McEvoy taught me
for that early self-portrait
but a few careful flecks, an impression,
an illusion, almost, of substance,
but placed with the utmost care:
the bodily weight of the sitter
conveyed by those shadowy planes
as defined by the arc of the cat
whose foundations are in the clasped hands:
confining the body from floating
off with our thoughts and away;
keeping it down to our level,
holding it down on the floor.

Held down by all that is round us,
pinioned by yesterday's failures,
pressed with the old indecisions,
the weight of our frailties and errors,
just like a witch or a vile one,
racked by our own misconceptions,

destroyed by the thoughts others have of us,
tortured with painful remembrances,
ourselves our cruellest inquisitors,
we are held in our places, kept
to our course by those burdens, those pressures
that most terrorise and afright us;
those things in ourselves, as in others,
that we try to forget or avoid.

Like the black cat on the lap
of the seated woman, the things
around us exchange for their own
something of our shape and image.
The window's the frame for our looking.
The window in us is the view.
Nothing worthwhile is accomplished
without a lifetime of looking.
The sketch is done without study
thanks to a lifetime of thought.

There is no one near me, save you.
There is no one... nothing... save thought.

Do I sound as though I am talking
from somewhere a great way off?

SHADOW

Waiting for the daemonic guest to come
in the dark labyrinth nine months of the year,
I seem suspended in an atmosphere
where nothing shakes the glass of claustral calm.
People are like shadows,
and I am like a shadow to them all.

My guide, my master, came but is returning,
the light within him answering to the light.
Led by him to this womb-tomb, I delight
in echoing creation and, discerning
shadow leap within shadow,
discover in darkness some light for the soul.

I accept the niche to which my life's consigned me,
seeing the light-shaft's nethery uniqueness
illuminate this cramping space and bleakness
with the unearthly glow by which you find me,
and watching, as at Lascaux,
the shadow draw with light upon the wall.

He I awaited turns as though eloping;
looks upward to some other; has turned round.
I, too, have turned away from the known ground
of hoping and, like him, gone upward, groping
but by a different tunnel,
drawing the shadow round me like a shawl.

NARCISSUS

arm
upraised
slender
braceleted
as though
about
to salute
the hair-braids
as though
about
to offer
a gesture to the noonlight
a caress to the stranger

the other
held
discreetly
behind
the folds
of the dress
the folds that fall
flood from the hips
flower
below the stem-
like waistband
below the banded yoke
and the broad belt, buttoned

the corolla unfolds, curls
crisp from the sheath

the shoulders
under the slim strap
torn by the stare
like a sharp flint
of the stranger
turn
to the sculptor's creamy stone

under
your gaze
I become
narcissus
a youth
wrapt
in wonderment
at his
own body –
and yours

numb
anaesthetised
I am altered
I become
yours
discreetly

I offer
myself
but never
completely

I offer
myself
but I am never taken –
being never alive
and never undertaken

I never
become yours
but I move,
sway, ever
so slightly, lightly
in the noonlight

I go on
saluting you
and the mirror, looking

I go on
tilting
my noon-dressed, sun-
stressed tingling body
to you

I go on
echoing
you, tilted
to you
in a kind
of talking
even if
unseen

arm
upraised
to you

eyes
half-turned
to you

don't go, don't turn away

stranger, sweet stranger,
don't go, not for the world

don't, don't turn away

go on with your looking

HERMES

What message, quiet one, from the other side
of window-glass and feathers? Is it the cold
that hurts you most or our effrontery
at working on and on whilst you are dying?
Do you know what's happening to you? What are you trying
to explain by the silence and to offer me
with a god's submissiveness? Your word will unfold
like Lazarus from the other and silent side.

DARK LISTENING

the flute
        calling through the darkness
flips like light through a lamp-black coal-dark cave
beckoning, accompanying our going
through the corridors
leading to Elysium or Hell

beckoning, accompanying our passage
through the anxieties and the pains of darkness
that confront us
like so many passages, all of which are leading,
unknown as they themselves are, to the unknown:
through which, within their winding,
the traveller through the darkness
is led, is guided onwards, by his hearing –
within himself or just ahead of him –
those sharp, quick beck-notes, bright like children playing:
seeing, round him, the darkness
but hearing only one thing:
together, yet one to the other,
the flute and the darkness, calling

There is no other image
that he, the interior traveller,
eyes shut fast, is knowing.

There is no other music
                        There
is no other way there
                        There
is no other there, other than that way

that way, through the darkness,
which seemed so solitary,
quickened, now, by the glimmering
of the flute
            beckoning
                  calling

NESTING

The wing flying upward, the chirp
then the shadow, the downward tilt.

Ah! Let the wing beat upward, the house be built,
the swish be heard ascending after the chirp.

When the protagonist flies...
whither? ...and bides... where?
is it in a land to the south, or closely and near
to my hand or my head that, awaiting Springtime, it lies?

Close to my hand, at this window,
it is here: it is under my eaves,
that the thought that is nesting within me enters and leaves.
The land to the south is within me, a country I know:

no longer far off, the dove's country,
because I believe in it,
the source of my spirit, beyond my spirit or wit,
where the wing flies upward in its absolute beauty,

through the seasons, and after them, bringing
my endeavours, my best ideas,
through the worst that must follow to what is after the years:
to join the elated ones at their winging and singing.

The shadow descending, the tilt,
then the wing flying upward, the chirp.

What I have witnessed, nothing can usurp:
ascending, trembling, I have felt the swish and the lilt.

from GREEN LEAVES IN A WHITE JUG

I

joy in a white jot, sunlight
in yellow and white
                        mus-
tard joy must
break up, out
of the musty mist's
moist umbrage, rocking
back and fourth dimensionally
                        out of the fore-
and background
to fire one
            shot
one fireball
            plop into the sun

III

Green leaves
                in absolute joy
jargoning, juggon-
ing, jumping
up just like a tumbler

not jogging along
                as we do
jagging our trouser bottoms
on invisible and visible snags
pointed litter, barbed wire
the wrong fences, encountered
                on the wrong pathway
climbed through
                in the wrong way
on the wrong day
                but springing up, leaping

                leaning forward
like a priest

                    to pronounce blessing
like a judge
                    to pronounce acquittal
like a messenger with a royal
pardon on tablets of clay

Green leaves
                    salute the jury, are
judge and jury, advocate and defendant,
and forgive us all, lift us
over the mist wall
with the certainty
cool
        bright
                    in its timelessness
of still lives:
                    live stills, of green
leaves in a white jug

                    trembling like a shot
held for millennia on screen

IV

Green leaves
                    in a white jug
evening colours, earth
tinges, looming
gloam light, containing
strong sunlight still

colour of a summer's
fine evening, fulfilling its day
with a promise of more to come:
more leaves, more movement, more travel
more sun, more water, more light

tomorrow waits us
                    blessed
forever

in this quiet-toned spray
though for some it means agony
                    dismay and disquiet

V

Blessed is the judgement
                    of this white jug
on its dun background
                    with its green leaves

Blessed is the green leaf and the dry
Blessed is the clay
                    in the hands of the potter
Blessed is the filled jug
                    solid, cool, the thirst-slaker
lightening held to the parched
                    lips of the juice-taker

Blessed are they who share this jug
                    and this juice
who partake of this life-giving gouache
                    water, honey, and gum

Blessed is the man who walks humbly
in the sight of this white jug
Blessed is he who abases
                    in the presence of these green leaves

                    in the silence of this jug
welling, spilling
                    running over with love
from the deep river
                    flooding through all our lives

Blessed is he who can see
in the life brought, pulsating, to a still
                    the presence
of the invisible
                    uttering
the unspoken

VII

the slender
        lengthening
                shadows of the lamp-posts
flex their muscles late on a summer's night

the shafts of late light
tunnel across the tarmac

up to the painted doorway
                under leaves

It is there that the traveller fades
              silently, like a phantom
to be discovered, in absentia
in the morning, by his actions, like good thieves

VIII

It is now night.
Black leaves are in a dark jug
against a musty blackcloth.

Outline is lost in shadow.
Only a faint moisture
        a slight, faint emanation
        of grass, hedgerow and woodland
catches hold of our senses
in the bedroom where we lie wakeful
putting what we can together: word, and more
than word, making this poem; sending
the images into the moonlight two by two

putting light and light together
        making night

putting jug and leaves
putting one and one together
        making for
the invisible doorway

blackcloth drops back
  releasing the fold that blinds us

putting night and night together
  making light

TREES

Trees leave thumbprints on sky
smudged in the memory: wind
battles with stillness of mind.

The feel of the thing: those leaves
against that overcast sky
are waiting for something to happen.

The door of light, as it waves
through the trees as they heave, is drawing
nearer then further away.

The dark-brown mould, the grasses
rained on, the damp-black earth
open and shut it from mind.

THE BLUE WINDOW

Through dark washes, the blue window
in the Rue Terre Neuve, Meudon.

Passers-by, far below,
are caught in its webs and undone.

Surely, not by Miss John
whose tight button we know?

A chimney-like thread of abandon
still twitches with unmixed yellow.

TWILIGHT: MEUDON

Sitting or scurrying, a term comes to our worrying,
whether we're termed a pedestrian or a dancer.
Look at them, lovely in sunlight, each of them hurrying
into oblivion, as though unequal to day-time:
quivering like the shadows on these walls,
transient as the twilight that now falls.
From my childhood on, I've seen them hurrying.
I've hurried myself, and been buried in the sands,
asking the questions I hold and now turn in my hands.
Oh, for a glance, in all innocence, at the answer.

The way the light curls back from the curtain-fold;
the light that is ricochetting off the ceiling,
is all I am sure of that the future will hold —
as though through impasto the brightness of yellow was glancing —
is the only sort of an answer coming my way;
is enough, like the sway of a fencer: my prayer's that it stay.
Sat by this window, only my thoughts stand the cold
as my life passes. Out in the street, they are scurrying,
thinking they know the full nature of what they are carrying.
Oh, for a glance, in all innocence, at its revealing.

MOTHER SUPERIOR

Come here,
Mother.
You can't
fool me
with that
solemn
look. You
are laugh-
ing, though
as in-
teri-
or as
they come.
Do they
come? Yes,
from crad-
le to
grave, to
meet you
all or
half way
and some
hope to
go on
in the
other
sphere, both
super-
ior
and in-
teri-
or, if
you see
what I
mean there
as well
as each
other.
See it

and say
it. You
are a
holy
woman
and should
know. Go
on with
you, there
and here.

SITTERS

They are but figures I use to tot my sum.
None of them exists unless I let her,
but at my call they come.
An unassertive character is better
than piquancy in the sitter.
Let them be silent or dumb.

Like puppets they must move when I direct them;
adapt their mood to fit what mine is, then.
Their right to an ahem
depends upon my saying them amen.
The one I choose must lean,
squat, or twist to my theme.

Out of the window slips serenity
when in they tramp, the unbending ones who, as far
from creativity
as their coiffure's pin, frustrate our vision, and are
insurgents, set to mar
intent with enmity.

THE SITTER

Tall
poor lean
the sitter
lean-
s her sides
at an ang-
le
of fort-
y-five de-
grees
to her
vestal thighs.

Al-
ways en-
thusiast-
ic,
lips quick
parted to
meet
the a-
live spirit
she
looks for
and merits

both
here, a-
mongst the oth-
er
quick, and
there when she
dies,
but as
to that she
is
not yet
half way there.

Warm-
ly sym-
pathetic
met
prayer-en-
veloped, en-
gaged
in a
dialogue
with
the Di-
vine One. When

I
want to
see God, I
look
into
her eyes, see-
ing-
beyond
her but cling-
ing
to her –
the holy.

She
the tall
poor lean one
knows
no bet-
ter than to
lean
there but
what better
mess-
age can
God utter?

NUNSCAPE

      none escapes
time's tight scrape

      Nun's cape
no escape

      nothing
is kept back
from those broad shoulders, nothing
from that broad-backed, broad-hooded sitter
from those broad planes of colour, independent,
almost, of their subject, and the light
falling on those broad plains, the broad
unsullied acres of the Nunscape

nothing is kept back, nothing
is added, although the world is added
nothing is taken away
                  sky
is in a back-room
is in a way of looking

                  un-
sullied,   un-
assailed,   un-
desiring
      Nun
aspiring
      Nun
uncarnally con-
templating, con-
ceiving
      bearing
one
      Nun sitting
quietly down
      hands
folded
      contemplating

otherness wholeness
sky windless while
wind-full mindful
of otherness, of other's scape
and scope, of others who escape
their scope, who find their scope done-
for in a dune-scape
           undone by doom-scape
agenbite of unscope

black-block, white
cape, almost no
back-scape
           almost all
no-scape, no escape
from no-scape. No,
not no-scope, not
no-scape, but inscape:
infinite-scape, offering
infinite scope, infinity of inscope

Nuns find hope-scope

cape
    cope
       grope
near to us
and to the wholly other
in nun's cape
           they act out
perfection nigh un-
to us
           daily
discovering the virtue in each other

none escapes scope
in this Nunscape

WINIFRED WITHOUT GLOVES

How are the high hopes, all
the ambition and laughter,
come to this shack, or marriage
in California?
We both went far, you and
I, Winifred, to find
ourselves, only with age
to learn that to corner a

career, no talent or strength
is enough, and gentleness
compounds the ill. Upstream
I swim still, defy tide
solid as a Welsh dresser.
Would we have made less mess
of our gifts if the teem-
ing spate spun us side by side?

Do *you* feel fulfilled, dear
sister? How can one know
if one is, when one's so
occupied in midstream?
One shouldn't ask, but clear
the rocks with a plunge, low-
er love into the flow
with a laugh and a scream.

Against the wainscot, stand
up and be counted, throw
your confidence against
fate, pit your hard-won calm
against the trend of things,
Winifred. Let your strength
make head in the wind against
indifference and alarm.

Bow like a trouper, toss
yourself into each piece;
rehearse like a maestro, merge

performer, audience, mood:
tackle the wild outside
the door and mould it, increase
the stream's scope by your surge;
stand in it and dam it, nude.

THE STATUE

Sun askant
the statue
but there is
no statue.
A monument
by Rodin
on the Thames
Embankment
might have been
of me
but there is
no statue.

This corner
of an empty
room
this basket-
chair
this paint
on canvas
must be
my statue.

Sun aslant
the *Cedrus
Atlantica*
inviting
courting even
statues
to the picnic
must be
my statue.

The sun arrant
on the hot sands
at Tenby
making
no mistake, leaving

the town hall in shadow
must be
my statue.
The light streaming
in at my attic
window
on the few
cats, people, I know
must be
my statue.

The sun
in Attica
lighting
the figs and olives
on their hot way
to damnation
bursting
in the thirsty
throat of the
statue
must be
my statue.

The marble
quarries, mines of silver
the hot paps
cats, sands, hot sunlight
on rooftops
must be
my statue
but there is
no statue.

Yet on the train to Dieppe –
the further I leave it behind me –
my life grows big, and bigger,
like a statue.
Apollonian
waiting still its carving

from the Dionysian air.
Look up there, in the sun there.
Isn't that a statue?

DIEPPE

is in a valley, is
bordered on each side
by steep white cliffs
at the mouth of the River Aques,
north of Rouen and north-west of Paris.

In the old town are
narrow streets whose houses
date back to the early
eighteenth-century. The fifteenth-
century castle was damaged in Hitler's war.

Closest of any
seaside town to Paris,
with its pebbly
beach and marine promenade, it became
fashionable in the last century.

Safe, deep, the estuary,
favoured by shipping
and the Duchesse de Berry
for a dash of the sea-bathing. Port and ferry
keep themselves busy. Fish leap on a trolley.

To this, her little and fam-
iliar seaside town,
came Gwen John, without luggage,
to die here, one September,
before the Nazis, black-sailed, bringing storm.

A child of Tenby,
pent in a big city,
suddenly she needed
with a sort of violent longing
to meet the rising wind and freshening sea.

In a valley,
confronted on each border
by the steep frame of her canvas,

the rectangle vibrates with light and movement
pointlessly lovely except as a reveille.

In deep, swept
out past the pebbles
of her altering meaning, she is swimming
out at the light end of the once-blind alley,
an Aunt Sally at whom the horizon's leapt.

TO DIEPPE: A LIFESCAPE

I

Picking up beautiful children
at Tenby, to draw and adore
on the sands, we stood looking
at the children, the sea, and the shore.

Our first studio in an attic
more starving together than sinning
at the Slade, when the mood took us
living on fruits, nuts, a sprinkling

of thoughts for our lunch in the courtyard
at Gower Street, under the dome,
plopped on the steps of the College,
— the first to admit women,

Nonconformists, or Jews —
freed to pursue the old knowledge
with a new pattern of lamp
over the grass, past the porters,

the wheels of trade, and brain's limits,
to a nightingale heard disclosing
the sinuous beauty discovered
by the midnight lamp as of old.

Yes, this is all of my luggage.
No, I can manage myself.
This war must not take too long.
I must catch the next train to Dieppe.

I long to wander once more
where the waves meet on the shore:
on the prom to stand looking
where the waves crest at Dieppe...

beneath the white cliff-edge to ponder
like Arnold — or Tonks, so afraid
no one would come to his show,

trembling at Millbank, late starting.

Unkind but unhappy professor,
he taught me to draw, nothing doubting.
His self-portrait had something,
but Augustus and Ambrose had more.

Anxious to get there, to Tenby,
Dover, the French coast, the Tate,
on the train I stand looking...
It cannot be far to Dieppe.

II

On leaving the Slade, I lived in a small room
over a mortuary in the Euston Road
and then, alone, in a cellar in Howland Street
making water-colours of cats. Then with my best friend's people,
I passed those months, my subterranean years,
in that dismal house where the shutters were always closed.
They paid no rates, but he taught me how the light grew
out of the damp dark. I did the self-portrait then
with its red sealing wax blouse: the confidence,
with the reservation and the hidden hurtness,
blundering out, in the strength of his technique,
with something approaching my joy on the beach at Tenby
or at high moments of the Mass. What did I do
to lose that joy, that confidence, that skill
when what I felt and painted were the same?
The beautiful weather comes, but I'm not looking.
The messenger calls, but I am not at home.
What I need is a trip to the sea, or something,
a bit of fresh air, and a few solid scraps of food.
Rodin was right. I was wrong to neglect my body.
Geminians need a plain and simple diet,
sunlight, fresh air, and plenty of sleep to restore them;
to replace their absorbed outpourings, the expression
of so much nervous abundance, the yielding of so
much of themselves to their art. They are always
fussing after perfection, locked in with themselves.

Art is a window showing us how we feel
confronted with reality, not how
we ought to feel but whether we are happy,
where death and illness do not interfere,
to say 'I am'. The more I live I discover
the infinite in me hungering for the finite
and not the other way round. But for the visible glory,
what is there to return to? All I ask
of God is already round me, and I'm happy.
Cezanne's are good, but I prefer my own.
'Your sister', said the master, 'has a finely
developed sense of tone.'
Thus spake the Whistler. I lived on that for years.

Ida Nettleship, Gwen Salmond, and I
shared a top flat in the Rue Froidveau.
I knew Rodin...well. Corresponded with Rilke.
Never met Proust. Attended Whistler's School.
Could only afford it in the afternoons.
'In that dress you look like a prostitute.'
'Well, father, I could never accept anything
from anyone capable of thinking so.'
Gave up my allowance, modelled instead...

grave dignity
            beautiful, slender figure
'un corps admirable'
            not as I am now

Dorelia came with me. Journeying
by way of Bordeaux and Toulouse
we made our way to Paris.
By boat, we crossed to Bordeaux.
On foot, we trudged to Toulouse.
Our first night in France
we spent in a field on the bank of the Garonne
and were woken in the morning by a boar.
It didn't need *him* to keep us girls amused.
Ate bread, cheese, figs. Fifty centimes a meal.
Ate in the fields and then bathed in the river.

Quiet-voiced, I reserved my admiration.
Pale, oval-faced, my hair done in a bow,
something in colour between mouse and honey,
I was slender of build, with tiny delicate hands,
yet I had a surprising strength for one who slipped
past you looking so frail. 'I shouldn't like
to carry that', a Montauban workman shouted,
pointing up to the bundle on my back.
I loved my solitude; became indifferent
to mankind as a whole, but passionately
attached to one or two friends; was apt to form
a strong attachment with them that soon cooled.

Dorelia, in a black dress, at Toulouse
reading at night, was waiting for the summons
of Hermes, or some more burlesque familiar.
Reading at night, facing the full lamplight,
she let her shadow lean upon the wall.
I painted her with singular tenderness
as though in pity for a being trustfully
unaware of the things that mar it all:
the scarring realities, those tendencies
in us that confuse and then destroy us;
the self-betrayal that must bring our fall
if we are not watchful. The rag of our tenderness,
though shaken as a dog might shake it by the wind,
hounded, torn in a night, is sacred to us,
haunted by what we cherish and must lose.

III

A handful of women
                Dorelia
Fanella
      a few nuns
a few orphans, myself,
an empty room, or a room
with a view and a few cats

Rilke, hold my hand

A beautiful life is one led in the shadow
but ordered, regular
            harmonious and ordained

Does what we can or cannot understand
have the most value, mean the most to us?

gradually abandoning the use of dark shadows
- the beginning with darkness, areas of black —
keeping my tones lighter and closer together

her tones grew lighter and her forms attained great breadth

delicate colours, emotional and spiritual depth

modest touches, extraordinary vigour

deeply rooted, hiding a world in her branches

a small flute, filling the room with its sound

IV
alone, now, often alone

alone, now, always

my only regular visitors, my pictures,
those I can remember and those I have by me

the self-portraits, the nun, the convalescent,
a young woman, reading
                young woman, with black cat,
nudes, trees, orphans, in church the backs of people,
Augustus, Ida, the shadow,
Rodin, Rilke — Hermes —
so many brush-strokes, and so many years,
yet all needed to express a single idea,
waiting for the daemonic guest to come.
That chair again, that table. Like a good-for-nothing,
I read, but am reading nothing.

For nothing, read shadow. Nothing is un-scape.
Nothing's devout, unless it's in the picture,
and it is in the picture, for the picture always comes first.

When I painted like that, my hands were full of flowers

prayers, letters
                meditations, notes on painting:
smoky corn and wild rose
                                O
rose thou art sick. Petals fall, smoke
rises, whilst we are looking. The invisible worm
is in the visible corn. The faded blooms
yield their strength to it, their thin bright reds,
seed, grain, reeds, collapse in their frames. Bring
nuts and nettles for Ida Nettleship
— as she was when I first knew her. Set
faded roses and vermilion
                        in a red basket, petalled
cyclamen and roses, straw and earth
                        (idea)
At night, I used to pluck the leaves and grasses
when the hedges were wet and misty in the darkness.
When I took them home, my hands were full of flowers.

misty
    devout
            but the picture must come first

Took no baggage,
but made all proper provision for her cats.

Tiny person, in black,
with her tiny hands and feet
and soft inaudible voice — the vehicle
of indestructible forces — dying
to the sound of the sea's smack
as it feels for the French shore
filling, emptying the crevices
                        rolling the pebbles
draining, straining the beaches

yet audible, always, in her indelible pictures
the idea of which can't be blotted out or effaced:
audible, and individual, in her piping
above the ferocious cacophony of lives
heaped upon lives, all
climbing over each other, all
straining to be heard
                    She, the quiet one,
has she succeeded where so many noisy ones fail?

How many shows in her lifetime?
How many books about her
                    in her lifetime?

The seas swell
            the waves swell
they crash continually
                    and, continually,
they are urging and concerning us
with their relentless surging
and their swell
How well do you know me?

                    Continually, they tell
their story, my story, your story, and hers.

                    It is a tale
of slow upheaval, of struggle
to rise as high as the first time
                                        they

capsize, subside, and fall
slowly, how slowly
                    only
to emerge resurgent, to break the surfaces somewhere,
to fly up in froth again, sooner rather than later
at play, as if endlessly
throbbing, ebbing, and flowing,
rocking with mothers and poets
as the sea surges and re-
creates itself, never quite fails
always trying, always trying again

never giving up trying

Probe me, try me, know me, pry me
open if you can. Catch me,
if you want me.

On the sands, at Tenby
as we stand looking,
we, my brother and I

on the sands, at Tenby
in the womb
waiting
waiting for whom?
Waiting for the daemonic guest to come.
What message, quiet one, from the other side?

alone, now, always

alone, now, as I always wanted it

alone, always alone

A CORNER OF THE ARTIST'S ROOM IN PARIS

Table with flowers by the window;
umbrella with shawl draped over
that familiar old basket chair.
She has found a different place for it,
cf. *A Lady Reading*
or *The Convalescent*.
If we will only look for it,
there's a different place for us all:
if we will only jump for it,
wrapping the flowers of our feelings
round us like a shawl.

The sunlight streams through the window
in just the same way that it always
used to, and will do, but something
has altered. One thing is missing:
the human presences. Only
artist and subject are missing:
meaning one person, Gwen John.
What can it mean? Has she upped
with herself to the window and jumped for it?
Someone has mended the window
if so. We can never be sure.

In any case, anyone looking
in at this corner of the artist's
room in Paris can see
that the tenant has been here lately,
is here in what cannot be hidden;
that she herself, if not visible,
is expecting to be back soon.

Only Gwen John is not missing.

Whenever we think of this corner
of the artist's room in Paris
she is in and through it all.

LEAVING THE CORNER

We spend our lives trying to hold the image,
our room, our world, our credo, clothes and books,
one passionate object and the way it looks:
one image of ourselves, the status quo.
The last thing we are wanting is to grow;
to go outside, where what we are may merge
into some shape our first self did not know.

Leaving our corner, we turn back again,
retire, retreat, return to it, at our will.
We who have been at home here, did not fill
the room with this crept fungus that now breaks
it down in sweat and rottenness and makes
disorder of the old wisdom. All our strain
's to keep to the corner furthest from the cracks.

BEFORE LEAVING

I
Well, then,
do you
know me?
Do you
see through
my enig-
ma? You
who might
have been
my son.

My good-
ness, aft-
er all
this lot,
you, of
all peop-
le should
have known.

Should have
known what?

II
I come
to fru-
ition
slowly
ah
slowly
because
I am
alone —

not because
I am shaken

with the
wind
but because

I am
alone —

not because
I am shaken
not because
I am not
as the others
but because
I am
alone

III
I tread
the grape
slowly
in the
grave.

What I
was then
am now
have yet
to become
will be
told you
when you
have arrived
where I am:
when you, too,
have become.

Have become what?

When you, too,

have broken
the mirror
leaving
the pieces
behind you.
When you, too,
after your journey,
have come.

IV

not an abstraction
in anything
I've done
yet, wearing
more of a mask
than any of them,
I move on, slowly
toward, not the finale,
but the further
goal: first
the child
then the
hat the
top and the
spider-figure
then only
the smile or
the sigh like
a frown
then a
bush, an
acorn, a
sapling
set against
oak

then
two
staves

one
higher
than
the
other
then
two
stones
then
two
stars

then

I
must
stop
now

and
then

NOTES

GWEN JOHN, SELF-PORTRAIT
Oil, Tate Gallery, c1899-1900 (Ref. John Rothenstein, *Modern English Painters*, Vol. 1, 1952 and 1976, plate 19, and Susan Chitty, *Gwen John 1876-1939*, cf. dust-jacket).

A LADY READING
Oil, Tate Gallery, c1898-1900.

SELF-AKIMBO
Self-Portrait, Oil, National Portrait Gallery, c1900.

AUGUSTUS, IDA, THE SHADOW
Photograph. Cf. Chitty – 32 – c1902, or Michael Holroyd's *Augustus John*.

MRS. ATKINSON
Oil, Metropolitan Museum of Art, New York, c1897/8. 'The sitter's identity is unknown' (Barbican exhibition catalogue, 1985, 82), thus the 'Camden Town' tone of the poem is but one possible interpretation, though it was probably painted in London, in Fitzroy Street.

DORELIA IN A BLACK DRESS
Oil, Tate Gallery, 1902.

ETUDES
A response to Augustus John's detailed and sympathetic drawing *Portrait of the Artist's sister, Gwen, seated*, done c1905/8 and shown in 1980 at the Maclean Gallery, London. The James referred to is the novelist.

DEAR FIDDLER
Portrait of the Artist's Sister, Winifred. Oil, Private Collection, c1897/8. Winifred had come to London to study the violin. Scarf and gloves catch our attention while, as with *Mrs. Atkinson* and the two early self-portraits, there is considerable strength and personality allowed to the sitter. Cf. the poem 'Winifred Without Gloves', below. The comment in the third stanza is from a letter of Gwen John's to Ursula Tyrwhitt, 4 September 1912(?), Barbican catalogue, 12 & 51.

CHLOE BOUGHTON-LEIGH
Oil, Tate Gallery, c1907.

SELF-PORTRAIT NUDE, SKETCHING
Pencil on brown paper, 1907/9. National Museum of Wales, exhibition catalogue, 1976.

TO RODIN: THE WAVES
Based on a phrase in a letter to her from Rodin, dated 1906.

CREDO
What she might have written, sometime between 1906 and 1913, or shortly afterwards, when she had become a Catholic.

COMPOSITION
In a letter to Rodin she mentions her feeling is 'profonde' and asks: 'Why have I made you my master?' In another letter, probably written much later, she writes: 'My religion and my art are my life.'

YOUNG WOMAN WITH BLACK CAT
Oil, Tate Gallery, c1914/5.

A NUDE GIRL
Oil, Tate Gallery, c1917? Archetypically, almost triumphantly, victim (hence this poem) or simply pathetic (hence the next in the sequence).

NUDE GIRL II
See the comment above.

STUDY OF A SEATED NUDE GIRL
Oil sketch on chalk ground, National Museum of Wales, Cardiff, c1907/9?

TO VERA OUMANÇOFF
Vera Oumançoff was the niece of Jacques Maritain, the Neo-Thomist philosopher. CF. the letters in *Chiaroscuro* by Augustus John, pp. 252/3.

THE CONVALESCENT
Oil, Tate Gallery, dated (variously) '1915', 'before 1924' and '1925/30'. Cf. Chitty, p.81.

GWEN JOHN TALKING
The spirit of the poem is drawn from a quotation in John Rothenstein's memoir.

SHADOW
'A beautiful life', she wrote, 'is one led... in the shadow, but ordered, regular, harmonious.'

GREEN LEAVES IN A WHITE JUG
Former title of *Ivy Leaves in a White Jug*, gouache and pencil, National Museum of Wales, Cardiff, c1920s.

TREES
Gouache, in the Cardiff collection.

THE BLUE WINDOW
Gouache, *Rue Terre Neuve, Meudon* (Chitty, 193) in the Cardiff Gallery. It is like *Trees* in being painted in a much freer manner than we normally associate with Gwen John.

MOTHER SUPERIOR
Cardiff, oil. *Mère Poussepin seated at a table*, c. late 1920s? 'She did nothing better,' John Rothenstein writes, 'than her best portraits of these nuns... in which her uncompromising search for visual truth is beautifully balanced by her affection for her friends.' (Cf. Chitty, 145.)

SITTERS
'We have not much to do with people... nothing directly', Gwen John wrote. (Cf. Cardiff catalogue introduction.)

NUNSCAPE
Oil, Tate Gallery, c1920/30, and entitled *The Nun*, this is the other portrait which John Rothenstein had principally in mind in his remark above. It allies a preoccupation with formal considerations with a sense of spiritual repose.

WINIFRED WITHOUT GLOVES
Gwen John, at 62, ponders her portrait of her sister Winifred, *with* gloves, c1897/8. Cf. 'Dear Fiddler', above.

THE STATUE
Rodin used Gwen John as a model for a memorial to Whistler proposed for erection on the Thames Embankment, but the figure was rejected and consigned to neglect in a shed. A copy of the *Burghers of Calais* took its place.

TO DIEPPE: A LIFESCAPE
The story of Gwen John's life, in this four section poem, is intended as a narrative/reflective ground-bass to the sequence. It is greatly indebted to John Rothenstein's memoir in the first volume of his *Modern English Painters*, and with his generous consent it draws freely upon it.

A CORNER OF THE ARTIST'S ROOM IN PARIS
Oil, c1900/5 (Rothenstein, pl.18); 1907 (Chitty, 65), Graves Art Gallery, Sheffield.

BEFORE LEAVING
A closing meditation, it points to the beginning, embodying questions that arise throughout the sequence.

AUTHOR'S NOTE TO THE REVISED EDITION

For this revised (and paperback) edition I have made no changes to the order of the original poems, and none of the original poems has been omitted. Four poems, 'Gwen John: Self Portrait', 'Augustus, Ida, The Shadow', 'To Rodin: The Waves', and the title poem, have been slightly reduced. Even slighter changes have been made to 'Nunscape' and 'Mother Superior'. To these 36 poems I have added four further poems: 'Dear Fiddler' and 'Winifred Without Gloves', both relating to the artist's early oil of her violinist sister; 'Mrs. Atkinson', relating to another oil of circa 1897/8 vintage; and specimens of my response to *Green Leaves In A White Jug*, the former title of the gouache and pencil sketch *Ivy Leaves In A White Jug* in the National Museum of Wales, Cardiff. The full text of this response, first published in 1982, is to be found in my book *Leaving The Corner*, 1992. The other three 'new' poems are published here for the first time. The first edition of *Gwen John Talking* was published in 1985 and has been out of print for some while. The direct result of Stride's willingness to undertake a new edition is in the two poems on the Winifred portrait, on which I had always wished to write. Whether they indicate a different perspective, or 'writer', I leave it to the reader to decide; but that they are different in tone from my response to the work of Francis Bacon (and other influences) in *Jack o'Lent*, or to Dutch painting, or the Impressionists and Surrealists, elsewhere, would, I think, be acknowledged as appropriate.

I am indebted to Sir John Rothenstein, Michael Holroyd, Dr. Alison Thomas, Ben and Sara John, Denis Clarke-Hall, John Cooper (National Portrait Gallery), Susan Lady Chitty, Cecily Langdale and David Fraser Jenkins, Margaret Pearce, Rupert Loydell, Nia Taylor, Helena Caletta, David and Margaret Hanley; the Trustees of the National Museum of Wales, Cardiff, the Barbican Gallery, the National Portrait Gallery, and the Tate Gallery, London, respectively; and herewith acknowledge my appreciation of the help and encouragement received from them.

It was only in the 1980s that Gwen John came into her own. When in the 1970s I first sought out her work, the Tate's pictures and drawings by her were still in the vaults, and the Portrait Gallery's self-portrait was in an office or corridor. Needless to say, both galleries granted me the fullest access to her work (and to that of Tonks and Ethel Walker) thus making possible the present book and facets of my fiction.

Brian Louis Pearce
Twickenham, February 1996

Produced by Bookchase
Printed in Spain
L.D. SE-5316-2004